W·   ·   ıry

D1281499

Keeping Unusual Pets

LIZARDS

Peter Heathcote

Heinemann Library
Chicago, Illinois

© 2004 Heinemann Library,

a division of Reed Elsevier Inc.

Chicago, Illinois

Customer Service 888-454-2279

Visit our website at www.heinemannlibrary.com

All rights reserved. No part of this publication may be reproduced or transmitted in any form or by any means, electronic or mechanical, including photocopying, recording, taping, or any information storage and retrieval system, without permission in writing from the publisher.

Designed by Ron Kamen and Celia Floyd

Photo research by Rebecca Sodergren

Originated by Dot Gradiations Limited

Printed in China by WKT Company Limited

08 07 06 05 04

10 9 8 7 6 5 4 3 2 1

Library of Congress Cataloging-in-Publication Data

Heathcote, Peter.

Lizards / Peter Heathcote.

    v. cm. -- (Keeping unusual pets)

Includes bibliographical references and index.

Contents: What is a lizard? -- Lizard facts -- Is a lizard for you? -- Choosing a bearded dragon -- What do I need --Caring for your lizard -- Can we make friends -- Fun time together --

Keeping my lizard healthy -- Some health problems -- Keeping records-- When a lizard dies.

  ISBN 1-40340-827-0

  1. Lizards as pets--Juvenile literature. [1. Lizards as pets. 2.Pets.] I. Title. II. Series.

SF459.L5 H43 2004

639.3'95--dc22

Junoy
J

2003015538

Acknowledgements

The publisher would like to thank the following for permission to reproduce photographs:

Bruce Coleman/Animal Ark: p. 6 (top); Bruce Coleman/Kim Taylor: p. 22; FLPA/Silvestris Fotoservice: p. 11; Maria Joannou: p. 45 (bottom); NHPA: p. 9 (bottom); NHPA/Daniel Heuclin: pp. 5 (bottom), 40 (bottom); NHPA/J&A Scott: p. 4; NHPA/Karl Switak: p. 35 (bottom); OSF/Brian Kenney: p. 11 (bottom); OSF/David Fox: p. 5 (top); RSPCA/Stephen J Divers: pp. 37 (top), 37 (bottom), 39; RSPCA/Ken King: p. 19; SPL/CNRI: p. 36; SPL/David Scharf: p. 40 (top); SPL/Sinclair Stammers: p. 38 (bottom); Tudor Photography: pp. 6 (bottom), 7, 8, 9 (top), 10, 12, 13 (top), 13 (bottom), 14, 15, 16, 17 (top), 17 (bottom), 18 (top), 18 (bottom), 20, 21 (top), 21 (bottom), 23 (top), 23 (bottom), 24, 25, 26, 27, 28 (top), 28 (bottom), 29 (top), 29 (bottom), 30, 31 (top), 31 (bottom), 32, 33 (top), 33 (bottom), 34, 35 (top), 38 (top), 41, 42 (left), 42 (right), 43, 44, 45 (top).

Cover photograph reproduced with permission of Tudor Photography.

Every effort has been made to contact copyright holders of any material reproduced in this book. Any omissions will be rectified in subsequent printings if notice is given to the publishers.

No animals were harmed during the process of taking photographs for this series.

Contents

Some words are shown in bold, **like this.** You can find out what they mean by looking in the glossary.

What Is a Lizard?

Lizards are one of the oldest groups of animals alive today. They lived alongside the dinosaurs 230 million years ago during the **Cretaceous period.** Lizards are part of the animal group called **reptiles,** which is made up of several thousand different **species.**

Several characteristics make reptiles different from other animals. First, reptiles are cold-blooded, or **ectothermic.** They cannot internally control their own body temperature. If the air gets too cold, then lizards slow down and eventually go into a deep sleep. Second, reptile skin is not stretchy like human skin, but tougher and rougher, with no hair. This makes it more difficult for a lizard to control its body temperature. Lizards do not sweat, so they cool down in other ways. A lizard's body temperature will change depending on its surroundings. To cool down they move into shaded areas, and to warm up they **bask** in the sunlight.

Komodo dragons are the world's largest lizards. They can be up to 10 feet (3 meters) long.

Lizards' eyes, as well as their skin, are also different from those of **mammals.** They have no eyelashes to filter out dust in the air, but, unlike snakes, lizards can close their eyes. Lizards also have an external ear opening as well as an eardrum. They cannot hear sound as well as humans. If you call to your lizard, it will hear what you say but will probably not come running to you!

4

Your responsibilities

- Never buy a pet without first considering the good as well as the bad points.
- Take an adult along with you to the pet store.
- Never buy a pet because you feel sorry for it.
- Check that your pet is **captive bred.** By purchasing captive-bred animals you will not decrease the wild population. Taking animals from the wild means that fewer lizards are able to raise young and keep their species alive. Captive-bred animals are more likely to survive and flourish in captive conditions and should not have the **parasites** that are often found in **wild-caught** reptiles.
- Insure your lizard. Your local **herpetological** society will offer advice. Health insurance for animals means that if your pet becomes ill, you need only worry about looking after it and not about the cost of treatment.

A lizard's eye has scales all around it but no eyelashes.

Lizards love to bask in the sunshine. Sunlight helps them produce vitamin D3 in their skin to keep them healthy.

Lizard Facts

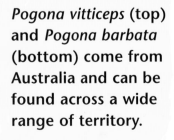

There are thousands of types of lizards living all around the world. They have adapted to life in very different locations with a huge range of diets and **habitats.** However, many lizards do not make good pets. The world's largest lizard, the Komodo dragon, for example, is an endangered species. It is in danger of dying out. For this reason, it is illegal to own a Komodo dragon.

Bearded dragons

Bearded dragons are one **species** of lizard that do make good pets, as long as they are well cared for. This book is mainly about bearded dragons, but the care advice applies to most other kinds of pet lizards, too. The **genus** to which bearded dragons belong is called *Pogona* and comprises many species, each with small differences. Two types of *Pogona* are *Pogona vitticeps*, the inland bearded dragon, and *Pogona barbata*, the coastal bearded dragon.

Pogona vitticeps (top) and *Pogona barbata* (bottom) come from Australia and can be found across a wide range of territory.

Lizards as pets

Before purchasing a bearded dragon, you need to consider its typical, daily behavior. Bearded dragons may be kept in a small group, but unless you intend to **breed** them, it is best to have just one. If you plan to keep more than one, remember that males will fight if kept together.

On introducing a cage mate, both lizards may start to wave their arms, as if they were saying hello. This arm waving, however, is simply a way of communicating with one another and helps them set up **territorial** claims as well as dominance or submission.

A bearded dragon waving its arm to communicate.

Your pet may occasionally puff out and darken its throat (or beard). This happens in both male and female animals and shows that they are distressed or annoyed. Normally, when the beard darkens, the bearded dragon will bob its head up and down to make itself look more impressive.

The inland bearded dragon grows to 8 inches (20 centimeters), snout to vent (this means without the tail). The coastal bearded dragon grows to nearly 10 inches (25 centimeters), snout to vent. Both can live for more than seven years, so owning a bearded dragon really is a long-term commitment.

Important advice

- Never put two male bearded dragons together.
- Never put two animals of different sizes together.
- Always have a veterinarian check a new pet before introducing it to another one.

Is a Lizard for You?

Before you purchase a bearded dragon you must think very carefully. Is a bearded dragon the right pet for you? Are you the right person to own a bearded dragon? It can be very disappointing when you realize that the pet you wanted is not a realistic possibility, but it is better to understand this before you buy the pet and make it unhappy, too.

Bearded dragon good points

- They can live for more than seven years.
- They can be handled every few days.
- They can be purchased as babies, and you can watch them grow.
- They need feeding only once a day.
- They need to be cleaned only once a week (spot cleaning should be done daily).
- They do not make any noise so they won't bother the neighbors.
- They become tame very easily.

Although they are not soft and furry, lizards can be handled on a regular basis.

Bearded dragon not-so-good points

- Bearded dragons carry diseases that can be passed on to humans (**zoonoses**) unless routine hygiene precautions are taken.
- They require artificial heat to **maintain** their body temperature.
- It can be very expensive to set up a bearded dragon's **vivarium.**
- It is sometimes hard to provide the varied diet needed to maintain a healthy bearded dragon. You will need to spend time and effort to see that your lizard has a good diet.
- Veterinary treatment is expensive, and finding a veterinarian experienced in treating **reptiles** can be hard. If your pet is sick, you may have to travel to find someone who can help.
- You will need to keep insects in your home, and there is a chance that some may escape!

Lizards like to eat lots of creepy-crawly live food. Are you willing to keep crickets in your house?

Some kinds of lizards, like this thorny devil lizard, do not make very good pets!

9

Choosing a Bearded Dragon

It is not easy to select a bearded dragon from a brief meeting at a pet store. You will have many questions that need answers. Most importantly, before you buy your new pet, stand back and take a good look around the store. What do you see?

Things you should see

- well-ventilated cages
- "guarded" heat sources protecting the animals inside from burning themselves
- thermostats controlling the heaters, so that the animals don't get too hot or too cold
- healthy insects for sale
- clean cages with fresh water
- **captive-bred** lizards with feeding records available
- **ultraviolet** lights

Have a good look at the lizards and the cage they are in at the pet shop before you buy one.

Problems to watch out for

- mites or ticks on lizards
- dirty water bowls
- dirty cages
- lack of thermostats or ultraviolet lights
- **wild-caught** lizards

One or two dragons?

It is perfectly fine to keep only one bearded dragon. It will not feel lonely or sad as long as you make sure that it is in the correct environment.

Male or female?

If you do not plan to **breed** your pet, then it is best to keep a single male dragon. Females can have health problems if they are not allowed to breed and may need expensive veterinary care if they are unable to pass their eggs. Remember, many female lizards will lay eggs even if they do not have a mate.

Buying your bearded dragon

The best place to buy your dragon is from a private breeder. If you have problems finding a breeder, contact a **herpetological** society. Society members may be able to help you. Always take an adult with you when buying a pet.

Top tip

Bearded dragons like cool, fresh water to drip onto their heads. It runs into the corners of their mouths so they can drink it.

Male and female lizards look very similar. Make sure you check what sex your pet is before you buy it.

Juvenile bearded dragons are very delicate and should be handled with great care.

11

What Do I Need?

A **vivarium** is a cage in which **reptile** keepers house their pets. You can buy one at a pet shop or make your own. In a vivarium you can control the warmth and **humidity** and make sure that live food cannot escape into your home. It is also important not to let a lizard run around your home unsupervised. Remember that reptiles may carry diseases that humans can catch. Also, your lizard may be accidentally injured by curious family pets.

Materials

Use wood as the main construction material for the vivarium. The front of the cage should have sliding glass doors (with toughened and rounded edges to prevent nose rub). This will allow easy access to the inside of the cage. Wood will help the cage stay at the correct temperature. Dark-colored wood will help reduce the effects of stress. All internal joints should be sealed with silicone to help prevent water from leaking out and to prevent an **infestation** of mites, which can **breed** rapidly in small gaps.

A wood vivarium with sliding glass doors is an ideal home for a lizard. What other things are needed to make the cage comfortable?

The wooden edges of your vivarium should be sealed with silicone.

Shape and size

Ground-dwelling animals, like the bearded dragon, prefer a vivarium that allows them room to investigate and move around, behaving as they would in the wild. A vivarium measuring about 48 inches (120 centimeters) long, 24 inches (60 centimeters) deep, and 18 inches (45 centimeters) high should be adequate for a single lizard.

Ventilation

The amount of **ventilation** in the vivarium will depend on humidity requirements. Vents can be made by drilling holes in the back or side of the vivarium. These should be placed at the top and bottom of the enclosure to provide airflow. Air holes should be less than a quarter inch (5 millimeters) in diameter, so that lizards and the insects they eat cannot escape. Vents should not be placed at the same height opposite each other because this creates a draft in the cage, which may lead to sickness.

Air vents like these allow fresh air to enter the vivarium.

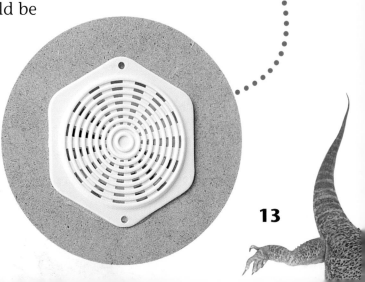

13

Heating

As an **ectothermic reptile,** your pet must have its body heat controlled artificially. You should create a warm area and a cool area in the cage. The warmest area, which your lizard will use for **basking,** should be 86 to 95°F (31 to 35°C). Place the heaters toward one side of the vivarium, rather than in the middle. Heating units are available at pet stores and online supply companies. There are three main types:

- Ceramic heaters: These get very hot and must be shielded.
- Spot bulbs: Use only dark colors. Bright white will distress the animal.
- Heat mats: These should cover less than one-third of the cage bottom. Your lizard must be able to escape the heat.

Safe basking areas are essential for your lizard's well-being. Notice that the heat source is shielded by a metal frame.

Cage needs

- a thermostat to control the heat
- a securely fastened guard over all heat sources to keep your pet from getting burned
- wire mesh that is small enough to prevent the animal from getting through the gaps in the mesh
- thermometers to keep a check on possible thermostat failures

Humidity

Humidity is the amount of water in the air. Low humidity can cause problems for reptiles when shedding their skin. It also can cause breathing trouble. Humidity meters are available from hardware stores and should be used to maintain levels around 35 percent. Remember that **ventilation** will change the level of humidity. An increase in ventilation will decrease humidity and vice versa.

What happens if the humidity is wrong?

- **respiratory** problems (breathing difficulties)
- skin problems such as blisters and infections
- eye infections
- **infestations** of mites, ticks, or flies

Check the humidity meter and thermometer regularly to make sure conditions are ideal inside the cage.

Lighting

There are three main types of lighting used for **reptiles:**

- **Ultraviolet** (UV) lighting encourages healthy bones and good muscle control.
- Reflector bulbs (combined system) can be used with other heaters in larger cages.
- **Incandescent** bulbs can be used to create localized hot spots and are available in a variety of wattages. For a 48-inch- (120-centimeter-) long **vivarium,** use a 100-watt bulb. The bulb must must be attached to a thermostat. The bulb should be placed at one end of the vivarium to make the largest temperature change from one end of the enclosure to the other.

Ultraviolet lights

Ultraviolet light helps many animals produce vitamin D3 in their skin, which is then converted to the active vitamin D3. Without D3 reptiles cannot absorb calcium. Ultraviolet lights should be left on for ten to fourteen hours daily and replaced every six to nine months. Check with a **herpetological** society for recommendations concerning the safest types of UV lighting.

Reflector bulbs

If used as a heat source, dark-colored bulbs can be used at night to provide a nighttime effect. Dark-colored bulbs can be used during the day along with a UV source to give a daylight effect.

Bulbs need to be changed periodically. Keep a spare one on hand.

If bulbs are used to create a "hot spot" then turn them off at night, as long as another heat source **maintains** the background temperature. A wire guard should cover all reflector bulbs. A pattern of day and night-time effects can reduce stress-related problems. Remember that your lizard will become distressed if it lives under white light for 24 hours a day, seven days a week. It is important to re-create the most natural conditions possible. In the wild, lizards experience a regular pattern of daylight and darkness.

You will need to move your lizard to a clean, temporary home before you start cleaning out the vivarium.

Hygiene

To prevent problems with **parasites**, make sure that the vivarium is well sealed with silicone. This keeps mites and their eggs from getting inside the vivarium. The vivarium should be regularly cleaned with a mild disinfectant. Pay particular attention to corners, and dry the cage well before replacing your reptile. After handling animals and cleaning out the vivarium, make sure that you wash your hands with a mild disinfectant or antibacterial soap. Food and water bowls should be removed, cleaned, and replaced daily. Do not place food and water bowls from the cage on surfaces in your kitchen because this may spread disease.

Use a mild disinfectant to clean out the vivarium. You must wear rubber gloves when cleaning.

Substrate

Substrate is placed at the bottom of the **vivarium** to absorb lizards' waste products. Some substrates are brightly colored to decorate the cage. Others, such as orchid bark, **maintain** high **humidity.** You should remove any soiled substrate from the vivarium and replace it completely on a regular basis.

Bearded dragons love digging, so high-quality substrate is essential to keep them happy and healthy.

Lizards live well on calci-sand, a product sold in pet stores. Be careful not to use sand containing silica, as it will **dehydrate** your **reptile** and can kill it. Bags of children's play sand are often sold as "silica-free" and are less expensive than specially produced sands, but remember to check the label. Any substrate can cause problems if swallowed by your pet.

Plants

Real plants look attractive in the cage, but check that they are not poisonous to reptiles. Plastic plants often break into smaller pieces and can be easily swallowed, causing a blockage in a lizard's bowel. Information about safe plant **species** is constantly updated. Check with a **herpetological** society for recommendations.

Green plants in the vivarium make it look nice and give your lizard lots of places to hide.

Cage furniture and hides

Furniture provides **hides** to help the lizard feel secure within the cage. It also reduces stress-related problems. Remember that it is your responsibility to help your new pet live a happy, relaxed life, so make sure it has plenty of hiding places.

Hides can be made from a variety of items such as cardboard boxes with holes cut in the side, plant pots, or anything hollow, even an empty toilet-paper roll! A heavy rock that cannot be moved by your pet also can be placed in the vivarium. Make sure there aren't any sharp edges, because they can injure your animal.

Hides are important in encouraging **hatchling** lizards to eat. If your reptile feels unsafe, it will stop eating. Hides should be placed in each of the warm, medium, and cool areas of your enclosure. Do not place the hide only in the coolest part of your cage, because a lizard will always choose security in the hide over warmth. It is best to place one hide in the middle, neither too close, nor too far, from the heat source.

In the wild, lizards often hide between rocks and cracks to feel safe from **predators** and to escape the heat from direct sunlight.

Caring for Your Lizard

There are several different foods that are suitable to feed to your bearded dragon. It is important to change your pet's food at different stages in its life. **Hatchling** dragons will eat a different diet from that of adults.

Remember to feed the insects fresh fruit and vegetables before you feed them to your lizard. Make sure you keep the box closed tightly!

What kind of food?

Your dragon is an omnivore, which means it will eat both meat and vegetation. Examples of live food include fruit flies, mealworms, crickets, waxworms, small locusts, and garden insects. You may offer small mice as a special treat. You can buy frozen mice at pet stores.

When feeding your new pet, also think about preventing diet-related illnesses. Make sure that the insects you feed to your dragon have been "gut loaded." Place the insects in a secure container with fruit and vegetation for at least 24 hours before feeding them to your pet.

Top tip
Never defrost reptile food in hot water. Place it in a sealed container in a cool area to thaw out slowly. A refrigerator is the best place to defrost your lizard's food items.

About 20 percent of your pet's diet should be greens.

Hatchlings

If you purchase a hatchling dragon (from birth to three months), then offer it small crickets (about one-third inch [9 millimeters] long) three times a day. Offer as many crickets as your lizard will eat before losing interest. These should be alive to attract the lizard's attention. Do not leave any uneaten insects in the cage. They will annoy your pet, because they will jump around your lizard.

Give your lizard many different kinds of greens, but avoid dark greens, such as spinach, because they upset the calcium levels in the body.

Food can be used to tame your lizard. Always use tweezers when feeding your pet by hand in order to avoid accidental bites.

Top tip

Avoid feeding mealworms to hatchling bearded dragons, because they are very hard to digest and may cause death.

Juveniles

Once your lizard is four months old, feed it less often. Try offering medium-sized insects twice daily. If your pet shows little interest in the second feeding, then offer food only once. Make sure that salad greens are offered every 48 hours, and never leave greens in the enclosure for more than 12 hours. As your pet grows, the amount of greens it needs will increase to about 50 percent of its diet.

You can offer your pet mealworms once it is more than four months old. Use a variety of insects even if your lizard prefers one kind over another. Be careful with the size of food you offer your pet. As a general rule, the food must always be smaller than the widest part of your lizard's head.

Adults

Once your lizard is eighteen months old, it is considered an adult. Adult dragons eat a wider variety of foods, including small mice, king mealworms, and adult locusts.

Top tip

Place greens in the coolest part of the cage.

Adult dragons need to be fed only every couple of days. Keep a close watch on your pet, and if it starts to look thin, give it more food. Record what food it is eating. Remember that its survival depends on you.

Always remove the back legs of locusts before you feed them to your lizard. They have a sharp piece that can stick in the lizard's throat.

Vitamin and mineral supplements

In captivity lizards may not get all the necessary elements of their diet. The most important mineral for bearded dragons is calcium carbonate. This mineral plays a role in supporting muscle **contractions.** It should be mixed into greens and dusted on insects you feed your pet. If you put a good-quality **ultraviolet** light in your lizard's cage, then no supplements will be needed except for pure calcium carbonate. Do not put any commercial vitamin or mineral in drinking water, because it changes the taste and discourages your pet from drinking.

Top tips

- Place a small amount of calcium powder in a plastic bag. Put insects inside and shake the bag gently until a coat of calcium covers the food.
- Remove the water bowl and offer the insects to your dragon. Once it has finished, replace the water bowl and return any uneaten insects to their cage.

A plastic bag can be used to mix up food and supplements.

Remember to place fresh water in the cage every day.

23

Treats

Waxworms are a tasty treat for a bearded dragon, but use these only as a treat and not as a daily food. Never offer cat food or dog food to a dragon, because it can cause liver and kidney damage and can kill your pet. An occasional spoonful of pet food will have no long-lasting effects, but it is best to avoid it.

Skin and nail care

When your lizard starts to shed its skin, spray a mist of warm water over it to help the process along. Once it has shed, make sure that no pieces of skin are left on its toes or around its tail, because these pieces of skin could restrict your pet's blood flow.

The nails on your pet will need to be cut regularly so that they do not scratch you when you are handling it. You can use a pair of ordinary nail clippers, but be careful not to hurt your lizard or make its toes bleed. Ask a friend to hold it still and only remove the very tip of the nail, usually less than 0.04 inch (1 millimeter). The nails will need cutting quite often. You can help your lizard file its own nails by putting rocks with different surfaces inside the cage for it to crawl onto and scratch.

Ask for a friend's help when trimming your lizard's nails.

24

Vacation care

It is never a good idea to leave your pet alone while you go away on vacation, even if it is just for the weekend. Always ask a responsible person to take care of your dragon. Pet stores and **herpetological** societies can suggest someone experienced in caring for lizards.

Checking your bearded dragon

Check your pet often to make sure it is well.

- Your lizard should not have mites or ticks on its body or in its cage.
- There should not be any unusual lumps or swellings, particularly around the mouth.
- Skin should not be stuck around the toes or tail.
- Its eyes should be clear and its nose should not be blocked.

The box that your pet travels in should be only slightly larger than the lizard itself.

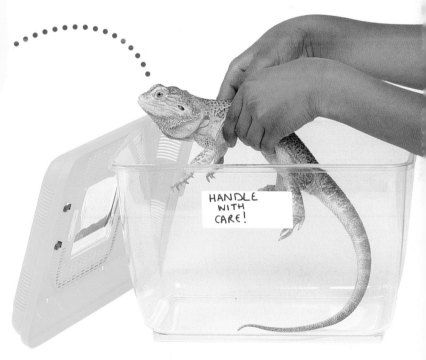

HANDLE WITH CARE!

Taking your lizard to the veterinarian

If your lizard gets sick, you will need to take it to the veterinarian. Place your lizard in a container only slightly larger than itself. The box should be strong, well-**ventilated,** and clearly marked with the words, "This way up." Keep the box out of direct sunlight and drafts, and never leave it unattended. Lizards can die in hot cars, so plan your trip to the vet well, and keep your pet with you at all times.

Can We Make Friends?

Reptiles are wild animals that have been bred in captivity only for a fairly short period of time. They are not as friendly as dogs and cats. However, most **captive-bred** bearded dragons are **tamed** from a very early age and respond well to gentle handling for short periods of time. It will take time for your lizard to learn your scent. Remember, lizards will not respond to you in the same way as many other pets.

Be gentle and take your time!

When you first select a dragon, remember to choose one that is healthy. Once home, make sure that you wait before you start to handle and get to know your new friend. For the first week, you will only be able to watch your lizard and feed it. It is tempting to pick it up and show it to your family and friends, but this will not allow it enough time to get used to its new cage.

Let your lizard get used to you slowly. Just watching it instead of picking it up will also help you understand your new friend's habits much better.

After patiently feeding and caring for your new dragon for a week, you may handle it for a few minutes. Gently lift it out of the cage in a warm room, and sit on the floor with it on your hand. Make sure you are in a room where it can easily be caught if it runs away. Time how long you have it out of the cage. Remember that it depends on the heat sources in its cage to keep its body warm. After ten minutes put it back gently and offer it some food. Never handle it immediately after feeding or you may make it **regurgitate** its food.

How to pick up your lizard

Pick up your lizard by placing one hand under its stomach. Then, supporting its full weight in the palm of your hand, scoop it up. Remember not to make any sharp jerky movements, because this may make it think that you are a **predator.** Never pick a lizard up by its tail, because this can hurt it.

Always support your lizard's body when you handle it.

27

Meeting other lizards

It is not a good idea to introduce your bearded dragon to other lizards. Unlike **mammals,** bearded dragons do not feel the need for company. They will not feel sad if they are housed alone for their entire lives. But if you still want to introduce your lizard to others, make sure that they are both female and of a similar size. Also remember that a healthy-looking animal can still carry diseases that are not yet making the animal sick.

Never let your pet meet animals such as dogs and cats. They may not intend to hurt your lizard but may think it is a toy and injure it while playing. Always make sure that all access panels of your **vivarium** are securely locked.

Be very careful when you introduce your lizard to another lizard—they are not used to having much company.

Always keep the vivarium shut securely, especially if you have other animals in the house.

Harnesses and collars

Many types of harness are available from pet stores. If you have a good lizard harness, you can take your pet outside on warm, sunny days. Natural sunlight is better than artificial **ultraviolet** light sources and will benefit your pet.

Top tip

Natural sunlight may change your lizard's personality. It may change in a flash from being friendly to aggressive!

Biting

It is very rare for **captive-bred** bearded dragons to bite their owners. However, a dragon may bite its owner accidentally at feeding time. Remember not to feed your pet with your fingers. Place food items close to it, but give yourself time to get your hand out of the way. If a dragon bites you, it will often let go right away. If it doesn't, try not to pull your hand away. This will cause more damage to the skin. Be patient and the dragon will let go after a short while. Make sure that you use a mild disinfectant on the bite once the lizard has let go.

Keep your distance when you feed your lizard.

29

Fun Time Together

Bearded dragons do not play in the same way as other pets. They won't fetch a ball, and they are very slow to learn new tricks! Some animal experts believe that you can train lizards, but in reality it is very hard to know when your bearded dragon is having fun.

It is important to give the lizard a high-quality cage and to change the layout of its environment once every few weeks. Have a selection of different **hides** and rocks. After cleaning the **vivarium**, occasionally change the position of the rocks. Make sure that you have a hide in the middle of the enclosure so your lizard will feel safe. Empty cardboard boxes and cartons will be of great interest to your pet and serve a useful purpose in keeping it stimulated by its environment.

It is very tempting to take your pet out of the cage for long periods of time whenever you are at home. But you should only handle your pet once a day at the very most. It is better to handle it only once every two to three days. It will not forget you or suddenly become unfriendly.

The arrangement of items in the vivarium can be changed to provide stimulation for your pet.

You can decorate a cardboard carton and put it in the vivarium as a new hide for your lizard.

Does my bearded dragon like to be handled?

It can be very hard to know if your pet wants you to pick it up and cuddle it. Watch its behavior. If it is bobbing its head or if its beard turns a darker color, then put it back in its cage. Reward your lizard when it goes back to its vivarium by giving it a favorite snack. But remember that lizards probably do not really enjoy being handled, although they may put up with it.

You can keep track of your lizard's behavior and how often you handle it by marking a calendar.

Keeping My Lizard Healthy

Before buying your lizard, talk with a few veterinarians to see whether they are willing to treat your type of pet. All veterinarians are qualified to deal with **reptiles,** but some may rather refer you to another vet with a special interest in these animals. This is something you need to consider, because it may be expensive, and the recommended vet may not have an office near your home. There are no special **vaccinations** necessary for you or your lizard, but it is a good idea to let your doctor know that you have a reptile, and make sure that your **tetanus** vaccination is up to date.

If you have a male bearded dragon, there is no need to have it **neutered.** If you have a female and do not intend to **breed** her, then this may need to be done later in life should she have problems laying her eggs. It may be difficult to tell the sex of your new pet if it is a **hatchling.** Do not worry—most single animals will be perfectly healthy without neutering. However, it is worth making sure that you know what to do and who to contact in the event of an emergency.

If your lizard is sick, you must take it to a veterinarian who will examine it and prescribe the correct treatment.

Can I prevent common diseases?

Most health problems in lizards are caused by poor care and cage maintenance. More than 90 percent of reptile diseases do not occur in the wild, only in captive animals. This indicates how important it is to give your reptile good food and change its **ultraviolet** light source regularly. Make sure the temperature in the cage is correct and that there is an area where it can cool down. It is also important to have your bearded dragon wormed at the veterinary office twice a year to prevent possible illnesses.

This lizard looks alert and healthy. Observe your pet every day for signs of sickness. Early diagnosis means early recovery.

This vet is giving a lizard medicine.

33

Zoonoses

When you take care of your lizard, be careful about keeping yourself healthy, too. **Zoonoses** are diseases that may be passed from animals to humans.

The best-known **reptile** zoonosis is infection by the **bacteria salmonella.** People who are very young, very old, or in poor health are most at risk for picking up an infection from reptiles. To avoid this, follow some simple rules:

- Wash your hands with an antibacterial soap after handling any reptile, cage, or accessory.
- Wear gloves when cleaning enclosures.
- Disinfect cages regularly.
- Keep young children away from reptiles and make sure older children are supervised.
- Keep reptiles and their equipment away from food-preparation areas.
- Clean bites or scratches immediately with an antibacterial soap or cream. If the cut is deep, see a doctor.

Wear gloves when cleaning the **vivarium.** Be sure to clean the edges and corners of the cage where bacteria can hide.

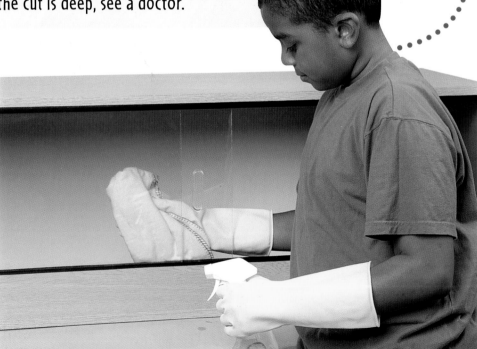

If your lizard bites you, ask an adult to help you disinfect the wound with antibacterial cream.

A darkened beard means stress. When this happens, it is best to leave your lizard alone in its cage in a quiet room.

Some Health Problems

Poor diet or environmental conditions cause most diseases commonly seen in captive **reptiles.** Many of the problems with pet lizards are not found in wild lizards. The more a lizard feels at home in a well-planned cage, the healthier it will be.

Ear abscesses

Ear **abscesses** are a common problem. The normally flat or slightly dented eardrum swells outward to form a bump. The cause is an infection within the ear caused by **bacteria.** The treatment for this condition involves an operation, so if you think your animal is infected, consult a veterinarian.

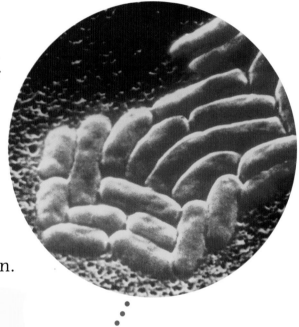

Infection of wounds by bacteria like these can cause abscesses to form.

Other abscesses

Any wound that becomes infected can develop into an abscess. Common causes include poor hygiene, overcrowding, and stress. If **territorial** animals, such as two males, are kept together with not enough space to form separate territories, one will attack the other. This may cause an abscess. A vet must surgically remove an abscess and make sure that whatever caused it is corrected.

Metabolic bone disease

Metabolic bone disease occurs when bones become low in calcium, which causes them to break more easily. Lizards may also develop a swollen lower jaw, weakness in the limbs (a healthy lizard should be able to lift its body clear of the ground), or loss of appetite. In the later stages, collapse, muscle tremors, and breathing problems can occur. Lack of **ultraviolet** light and poor diet are often the main causes.

If the disorder is serious, the lizard may need to have weekly calcium injections. Some lizards can have a moderate to severe form of the disease, although their owners may not even be aware that there is a problem.

Swollen legs are often a sign that a lizard has metabolic bone disease.

This lizard has a diseased jaw. This is another symptom of metabolic bone disease.

Respiratory disease

Signs of **respiratory** disease include a runny nose, sneezing, wheezing, labored breathing, and open-mouthed breathing. A simple infection of the nose can easily become pneumonia if untreated. Bacteria are the most common cause of infection, but **viruses, fungi,** and **parasites** also can be involved. Very sick animals require hospitalization for treatments such as fluid therapy and force-feeding. Milder infections may respond to antibiotics, a type of medicine that kills bacteria.

Many antibiotics are made for **mammals,** which are warm-blooded animals. You will need to increase the cage temperature or the antibiotics may not work. Some infections may be passed from you to your pet. If you are sick, ask a member of your family or a friend to take care of your pet for a few days to reduce the risk of infecting your pet. Keeping your pet clean will also help reduce any risk of infection occurring.

A lizard receives a dose of antibiotics from the vet.

Internal parasites

A **parasite** is an animal that depends completely on another animal for its food and nourishment and to complete its life cycle. All **reptiles** that are **wild caught** are likely to have internal parasites unless a sample of feces has been taken and no parasites were found. Parasites slow the animals' growth rates and make them more likely to get diseases. It is a good idea to worm mature animals at least once a year. If left untreated, parasites can cause death.

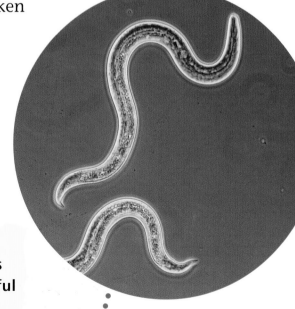

Nematode worms like these often infect lizards and can have very harmful effects on their health.

38

Veterinarians worm a lizard by giving it medicine by mouth or by giving it a small injection. The treatment is often repeated after ten to fourteen days. Lizards with parasites may have different symptoms, such as diarrhea or live worms in their feces.

External parasites

Parasites that live on the outside of your lizard are called external parasites. Mites and ticks are common examples of these. They are blood-sucking parasites that, in large numbers, may cause **anemia.** They spread very quickly. They also may contribute to the spread of other diseases between reptiles. These parasites enter the cage on your pet or on a piece of equipment that you have just purchased from a place where there is an active **infestation.** Always have your pet get treatment when it has parasites.

Ticks are fairly large and easy to spot, although they may hide in big body cavities such as the nostrils. Individual ticks may be removed with tweezers. However, be careful not to leave tick mouthparts behind in the lizard's skin. This can lead to the formation of **abscesses.** It is better to get a vet to remove ticks for you, though many experienced reptile keepers will have carried out this task and may offer to help you.

This lizard has an infestation of ticks on its tail.

Mites are smaller than ticks. They can hide under single scales. Large numbers of them may thrive on sick animals. Mites may be noticed crawling on the owner's skin immediately after handling the **reptile** or floating dead in the water bowl. Mites do not generally bite people. A single female mite can lay between 90 to 100 eggs in spaces in the cage. This means that treating the cage as well as the animal is very important. There are many suggested treatments for mite **infestations,** but unfortunately none has proved 100 percent effective and safe for both reptiles and their owners.

Mites are relatives of spiders and have eight legs.

Tail shedding

Many **species** of lizards escape **predators** in the wild by shedding their tails. If a predator grasps the tail, it will drop off and often twitch to distract the predator. This shedding of the tail does not harm the lizard. But it does cause some distress, so avoid grabbing and pulling your lizard's tail. If the tail is shed, it will eventually grow back, although it will not look identical to the original one.

Tail shedding is a distress signal. Never hold your lizard by the tail as it may cause your pet to shed it!

Treatments to get rid of mites

- Baths. Bathing an animal for about 30 minutes will kill most of the mites on its body, although those around the head will escape. The water should be about 77°F (25°C).
- Dichlorvos. Strips containing this insecticide may be placed in the cage according to the instructions on the package. You will need only a very small piece. This method has the advantage of treating the animal and the cage at the same time, but it can sometimes poison a reptile or its owner. You must remove the water bowl during the treatment to avoid this.
- Ivermectin. This medicine is available only from vets. It can be injected in very small doses to treat individual reptiles.
- Fipronil. This is a spray used as a flea and tick treatment for dogs and cats.

It is best to ask the advice of your veterinarian if you think that your lizard has mites.

A bath will get rid of most mites. But you may need to use other treatments to get rid of the whole infestation.

Keeping Records

To help decide whether your pet is growing healthily and developing well, it is important to keep accurate records on your computer or in a notebook. Over a period of time it is difficult to remember when your lizard was last fed or when it last passed urine and feces.

Make a note of whether or not your pet has been eating. Remember that if it does not eat for a few days or more you may need to take it to the veterinarian to be checked. There may be a reason it has lost its appetite or that eating has become difficult. It is very important to notice whether or not your pet lizard is passing feces. Blockages of the bowel are very common and life-saving surgery depends on your noticing quickly that there is a problem.

Remember to get your family to take photos of you with your lizard.

You can make a colorful scrapbook about your pet using photos, drawings, and notes about your time spent together.

42

Records can help tell you if you need to take your lizard to see the veterinarian. Take copies of any notes you made about your lizard's health with you if you go to the veterinarian. This information will make sure that the veterinarian knows what is worrying you and can help the vet identify anything unusual.

Keeping a detailed record sheet will help you maintain up-to-date information about your pet's health.

Example of a record sheet:

Species							
Sex . . . . Age							
Diet							
Frequency							
Temperature (day) . . . . (night)							
Photo period – 12 hours							

Key
Wt . . Weight
App . . Appetite
Th . . . Thirst
U . . . Urine
F . . . . Feces

Date	Wt	App	Th	U	F	What we did today	Carer

Also, why not put photographs of the two of you together at different stages in your lizard's life to make a scrapbook? You can take this to school and show your friends all about your pet and how you care for it.

43

When a Lizard Dies

If you give your lizard a well-designed cage, a good diet, and re-create its natural **habitat** to the best of your ability, it should live a number of years. A bearded dragon, for example, should live about seven years. It is possible for dragons to live longer, and as equipment for keeping them in captivity improves, they will likely live longer.

But no matter how well you care for your pet, one day it will die. Perhaps it will die peacefully in its sleep. If your pet is very ill, you and your veterinarian may have to make the decision to put the lizard to sleep to prevent unnecessary suffering. It is never easy to decide when is the "right" time to let the vet give an overdose of anesthetic to put your lizard to sleep. Part of you will always want just one extra day to take your pet home and say good-bye privately. But if your lizard is in pain, then as a true friend you will need to be strong and allow the veterinarian to end the suffering.

As your lizard gets older, it may spend more time resting.

Feeling upset

Whether your pet passes away in its sleep or at the veterinarian's office, you will feel upset. It is natural to cry when you think of your pet leaving your life. You will miss your pet. But after a period of time the pain will become less, and you will remember the happy times you spent together.

If your lizard becomes too weak due to illness or old age, you may have to make the difficult decision of putting it to sleep.

You can make a burial mound to mark your lizard's grave.

45

Glossary

abscess   soft lump filled with pus

anemia   illness in which the number of red blood cells is below normal

bacteria   microscopic life-forms that may cause diseases

bask   lie exposed to warmth or sunlight

breed   keep animals and encourage them to mate so they produce young

captive bred   raised by humans, not in the wild

contraction   shortening of a muscle

Cretaceous period   time in history when flowering plants first appeared and dinosaurs died out

dehydrate   dry out or lose enough water to cause discomfort or illness

ectothermic   depending on external sources to keep the body warm (cold-blooded)

fungus   (more than one are called fungi) life-form that gets food by absorbing other living or decaying material

genus   group of related animals or plants

habitat   place where an animal or plant lives or grows

hand tame   brought up by humans with lots of time spent in training

hatchling   recently hatched baby

herpetological   relating to the study of reptiles and amphibians

hide   place for an animal to take shelter from predators, sunshine, or rain

humidity   moisture in the air

incandescent   type of light emitted by an object that has been heated until it gives off light

infestation   presence of parasites in large numbers

maintain   keep at the same level or rate; keep in good condition

mammal   warm-blooded animal with fur or hair

neuter   perform an operation that keeps an animal from having babies

parasite   small creature, such as a tick or worm, that lives on or in another animal's body

predator   animal that hunts and kills other animals for food

regurgitate   bring swallowed food up again to the mouth

reptile   cold-blooded animal with scaly or rough skin

respiratory   having to do with breathing

salmonella   type of bacteria

species   group of animals that has the same features and can have babies with each other

substrate   soft material placed in the bottom of a lizard cage

territorial   describes behavior in which an animal defends space it views as its own

tetanus   disease that affects muscles and is caused by bacteria

ultraviolet   type of light that is invisible to humans and is used to produce vitamin D in a lizard's skin

vaccination   injection given to protect against a disease

ventilation   allowing air to enter and circulate freely in a closed space

virus   microscopic substance that can cause disease

vivarium   reptile cage

wild caught   captured from the wild

zoonosis   disease that can be passed from animals to humans

Further Reading

Bartlett, Richard D. *Lizard Care from A to Z.* Hauppauge, N.Y.: Barron's Educational Series, 1997.

Engfer, Leeanne. *My Pet Lizards.* Minneapolis, Minn.: Lerner Publications Library, 1999.

Schafer, Susan. *Lizards.* Tarrytown, N.Y.: Benchmark Books, 2000.

Zeaman, John. *Exotic Pets: From Alligators to Zebra Fish.* Danbury, Conn.: Franklin Watts, 1999.

Useful Addresses

The American Society for the Prevention of Cruelty to Animals
424 E. 92nd St.
New York, NY 10128
Tel: (212) 876-7700
http://www.aspca.org

National Alternative Pet Association
P.O. Box 369
Burnet, TX 78611
http://www.altpet.net

Society for the Study of Amphibians and Reptiles
P.O. Box 253
Marceline, MO 64658
Tel.: (660) 256-3252
http://www.ssarherps.org

Disclaimer
All Internet addresses (URLs) given in this book were valid at the time of going to press. However, due to the dynamic nature of the Internet, some addresses may have changed, or sites may have ceased to exist since publication. While the author and publisher regret any inconveniences this may cause readers, no responsibility for any such changes can be accepted by either the author or the publisher.

Index